GUITAR TABLATURE EDITIO

The Classic Songs and
Eric Clapton

Eight best-known songs recorded by the legendary guitarist.
Arranged for guitar tablature with chord names and full lyrics.

Fender Stratocaster on cover owned by Scot Arch
Photographed by William Draffen
Music engraving by Chelsea Music Service

Order No. AM 934318
US International Standard Book Number: 0.8256.1523.2
UK International Standard Book Number: 0.7119.5400.3

Exclusive Distributors:
Music Sales Corporation
257 Park Avenue South, New York, NY 10010 USA
Music Sales Limited
8/9 Frith Street, London W1P 3LA England
Music Sales Pty. Limited
120 Rothschild Street, Rosebery, Sydney, NSW 2018, Australia

Printed and bound in the United States of America by
Vicks Lithograph and Printing Corporation

AMSCO PUBLICATIONS
New York • London • Sydney

Legend of Music Symbols

I Looked Away

Words and Music by Bobby Whitlock and Eric Clapton

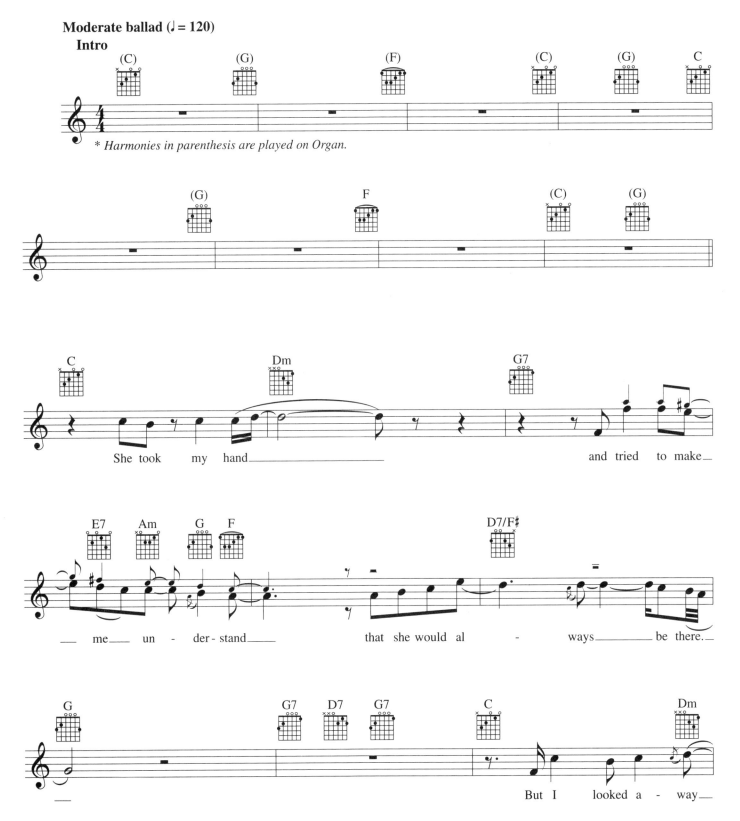

Moderate ballad (♩ = 120)

Intro

Harmonies in parenthesis are played on Organ.

She took my hand_____ and tried to make___ me___ un - der-stand___ that she would al - ways___ be there.___ But I looked a - way___

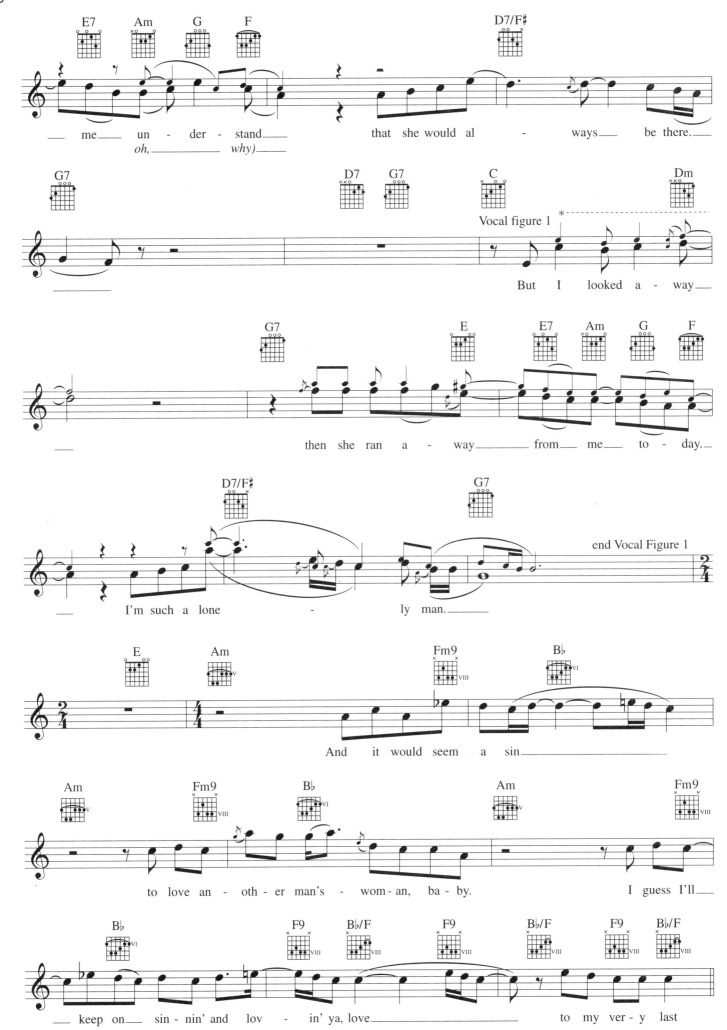

Guitar solo 1

* Use slight vibrato on each note
  for entire solo section (8 bars)

with Vocal figure 1

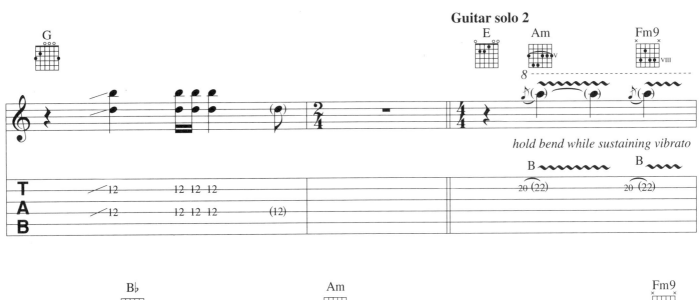

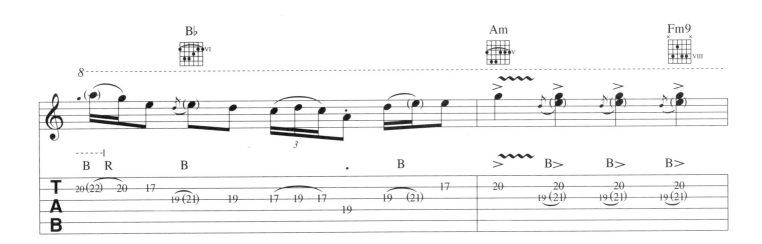

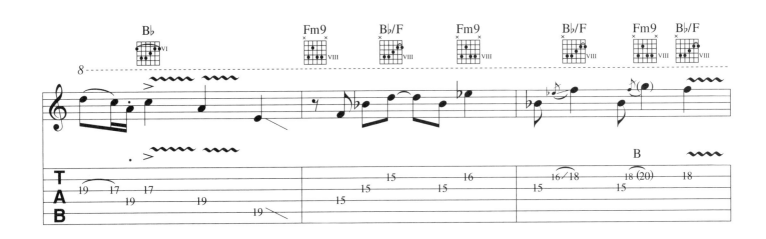

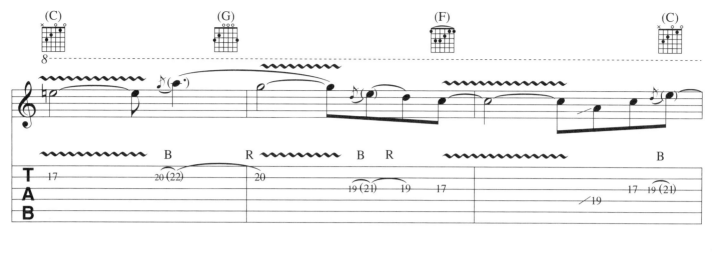

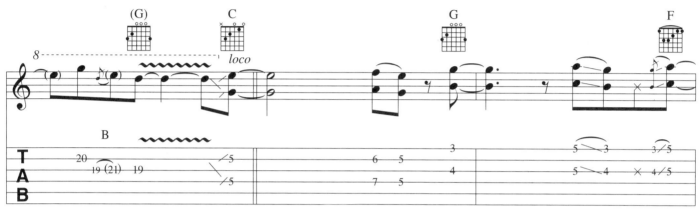

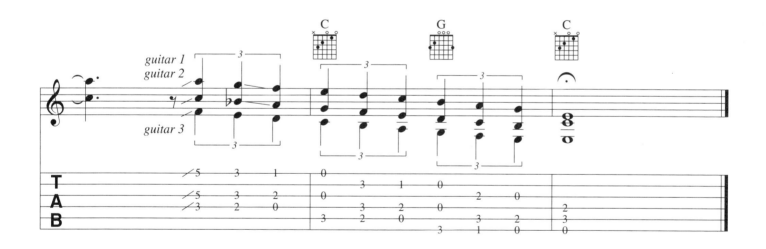

Tell The Truth

Words and Music by Eric Clapton and Bobby Whitlock

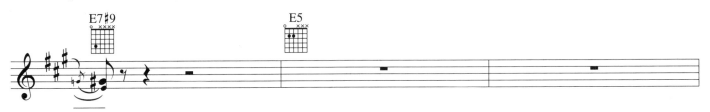

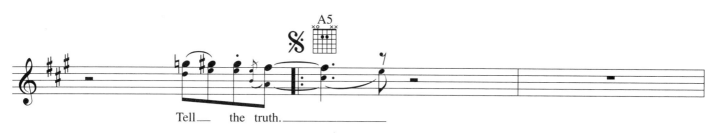

Tell__ the truth._____

Ah, who's been fool - in' you____ hoo____ hoo?__

*_____ * repeat previous 8 bars on 2nd & 3rd repeat only

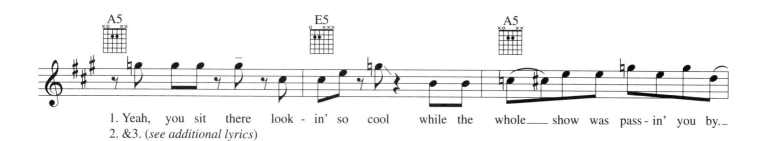

1. Yeah, you sit there look - in' so cool while the whole__ show was pass - in' you by.__
2. &3. (see additional lyrics)

_____ Eve - ry time you turn, you put

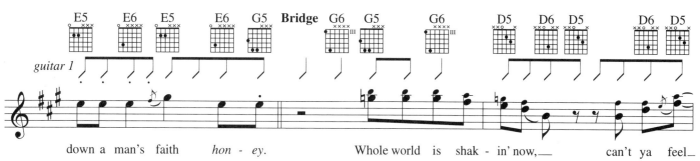

down a man's faith *hon - ey.* Whole world is shak - in' now,__ can't ya feel__

*guitar 3 plays rhythm fills in Open E tuning with slide

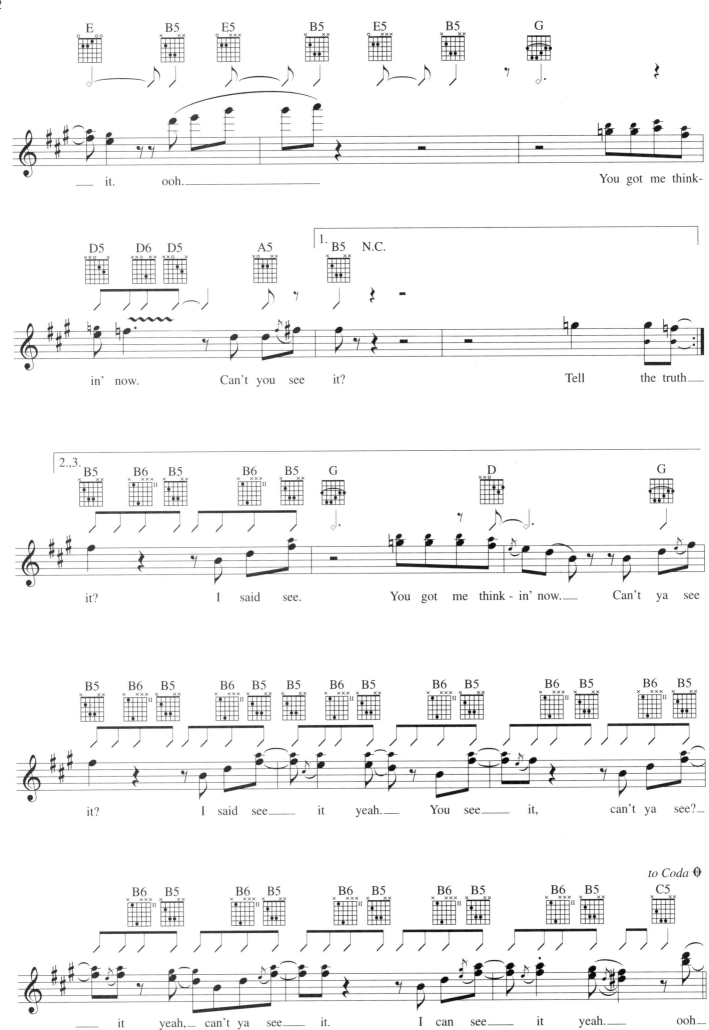

Guitar solo

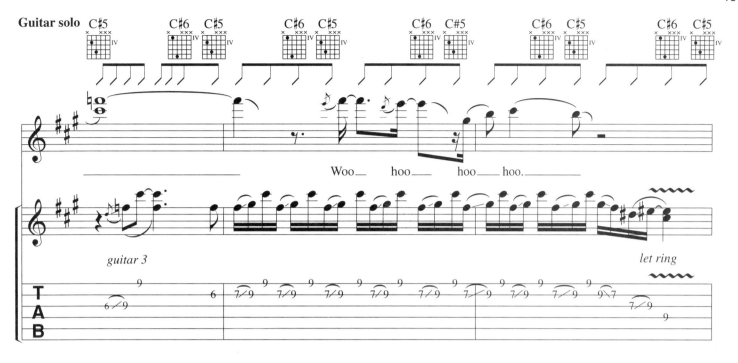

Woo___ hoo___ hoo___ hoo.___

guitar 3

let ring

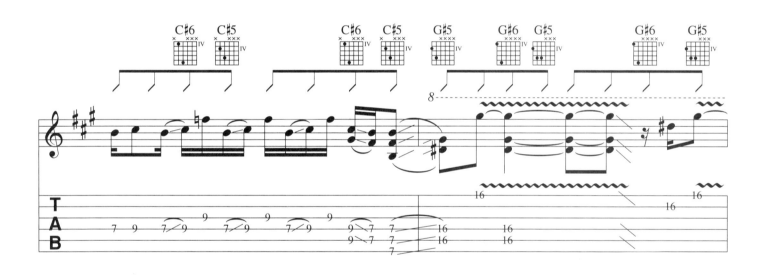

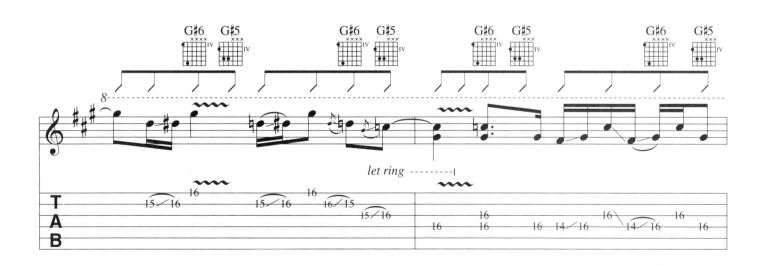

let ring - - - - - - - - - |

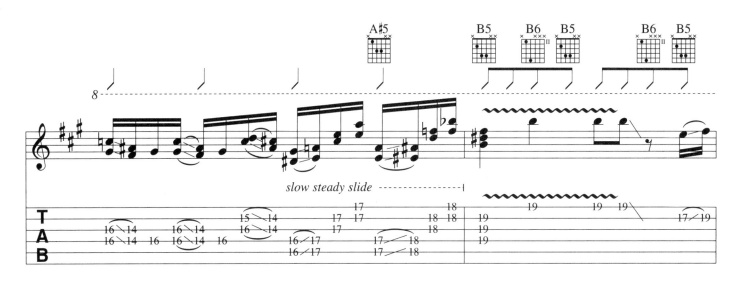

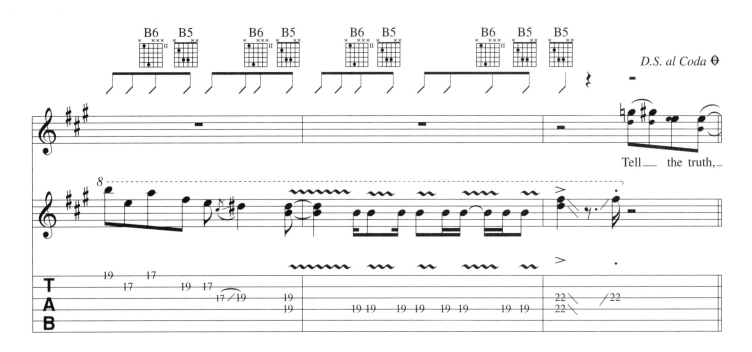

Tell___ the truth,___

___ it?   Can't you   see___ it? Yeah___   Woo___ hoo,___ hoo,___ hoo,

*guitar 2 plays ad lib fills

The whole world is shak - in' now.   Can't you feel___ it?

You got me think - in' now, can't you see____

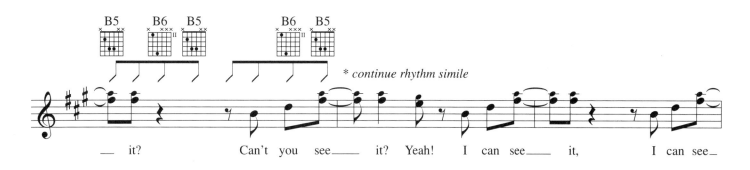

continue rhythm simile

____ it? Can't you see____ it? Yeah! I can see____ it, I can see____

____ it. Yeah! I can see____ it. I can see____ it, Yeah! I can see____

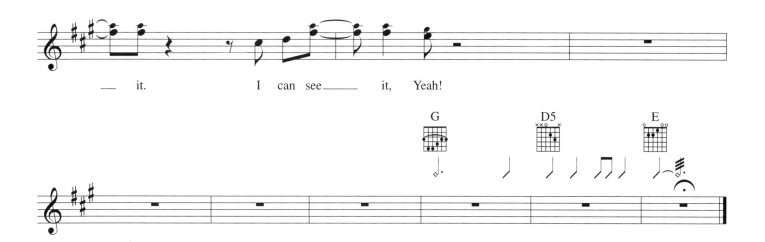

____ it. I can see____ it, Yeah!

Additional lyrics

2. It doesn't matter who you are,
   or where you're going to dance, yeah.
   Hey, open your eyes, look at your poor boy.

3. Hear what I say! 'Cause every word is true,
   God, I wouldn't tell you no lie,
   Your time's comin', gonna be soon, boy.

Crossroads

by Robert Johnson

take me   if   you please.___
ev-'ry-bod-y passed me   by.___
on   the   riv - er - side.___

I went down___
Well I'm

Guitar solo 1

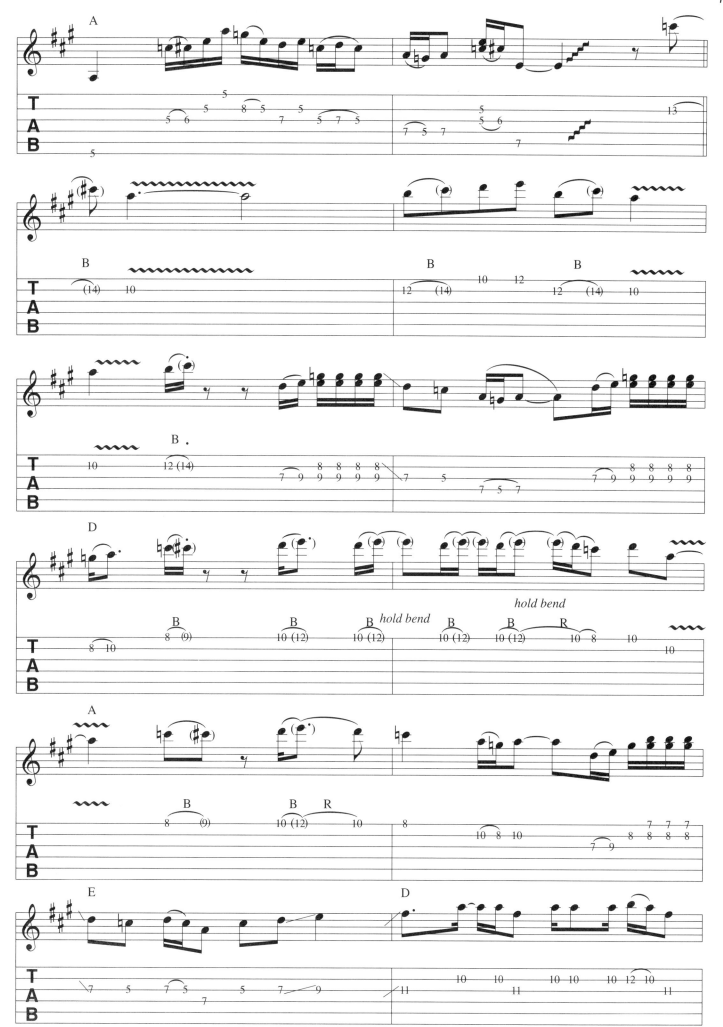

Cocaine

Words and Music by John J. Cale

Guitar solo 1

guitar 2 Rhythm figure 1 (three times) *simile*

If your thing is gone, and ya wan-na ride on, co-caine._

guitar 1

Guitar solo 2

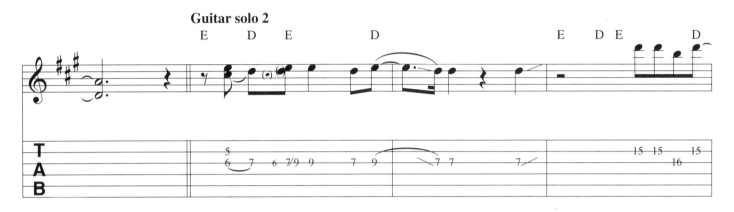

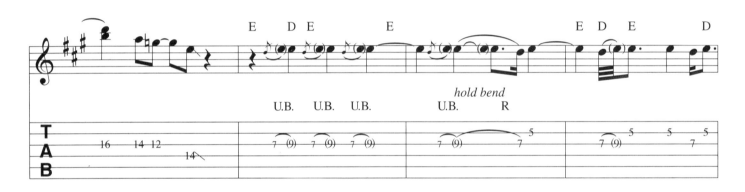

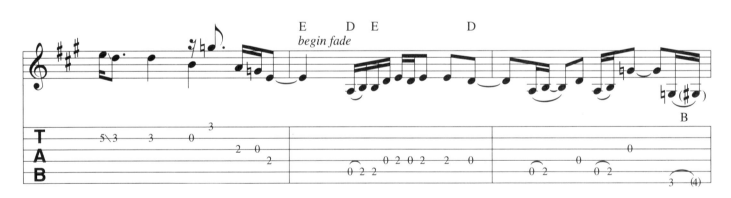

Comin' Home

Words and Music by Bonnie Sheridan and Eric Clapton

guitar 2 plays ad lib rhythm pattern

*on D.S. only

* guitar 3 plays fills with slide

to Coda

1.,2.,3.

4.

1st time only

Verse

Been out___ on the road_____ 'bout six months
Hitch hik-in' on the turn - pike all___ day___ long.__

Riff A   end Riff A

* guitars 2&3 play single note rhythm pattern

guitar 1 Riff A (six times)
guitars 2&3 continue simile

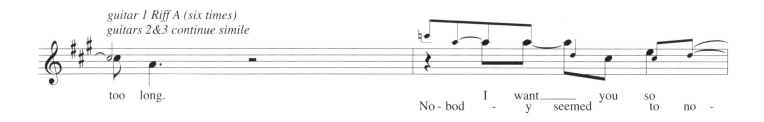

too long.   No - bod - y seemed to no -

bad,___   I can hard - ly stand it.
tice;   just pass me o - ver.___

I'm so___ tired,_____ and I'm all a - lone.
To keep___ from go - in'___ cra - zy,___ I got - ta sing my song.___

___   We'll soon___ be to - geth - er,___
___   Got a - whole___ lot of lov - in'.___

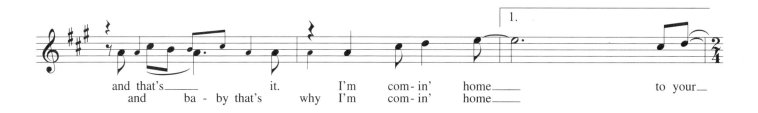

and that's___ it. I'm com - in' home___ to your___
and ba - by that's why I'm com - in' home

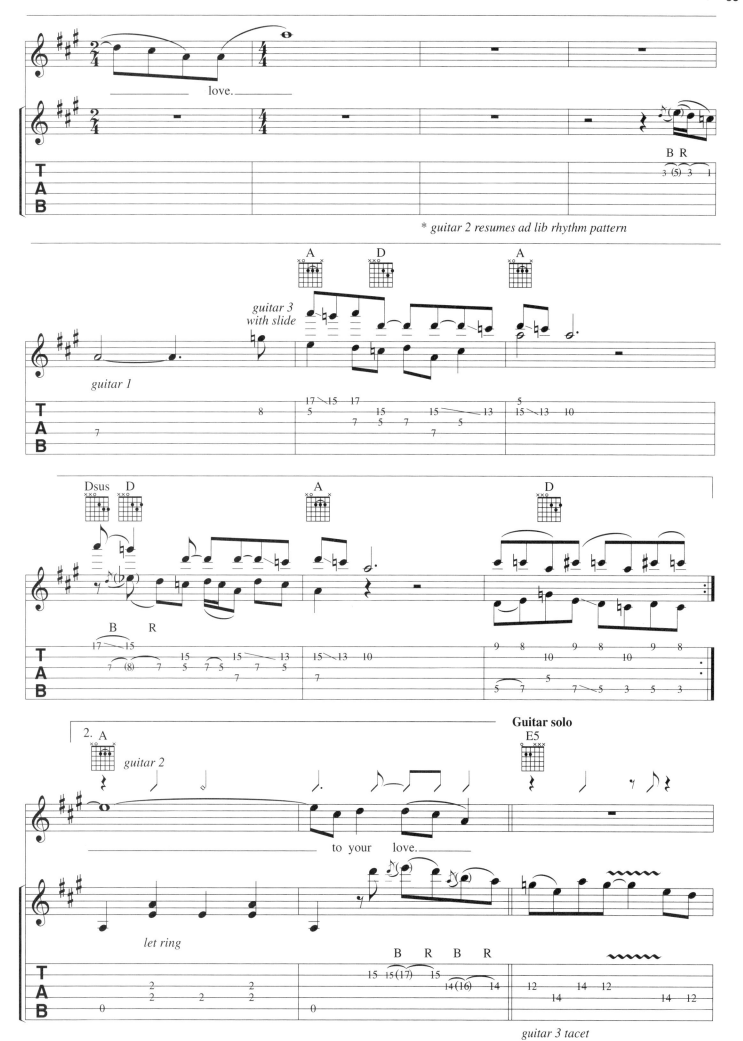

* guitar 2 resumes ad lib rhythm pattern

guitar 3 tacet

34

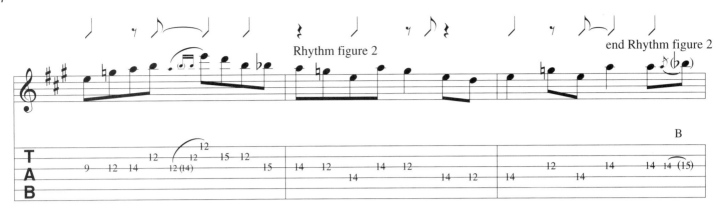

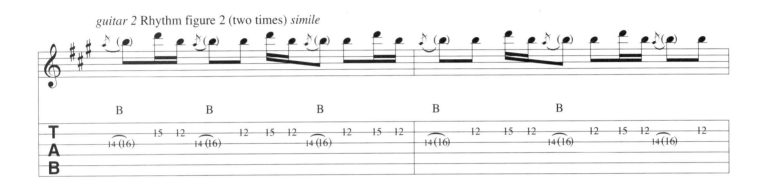

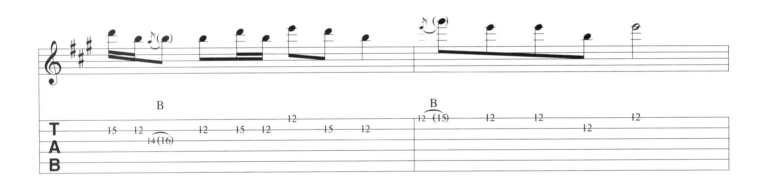

Com - in' home._____

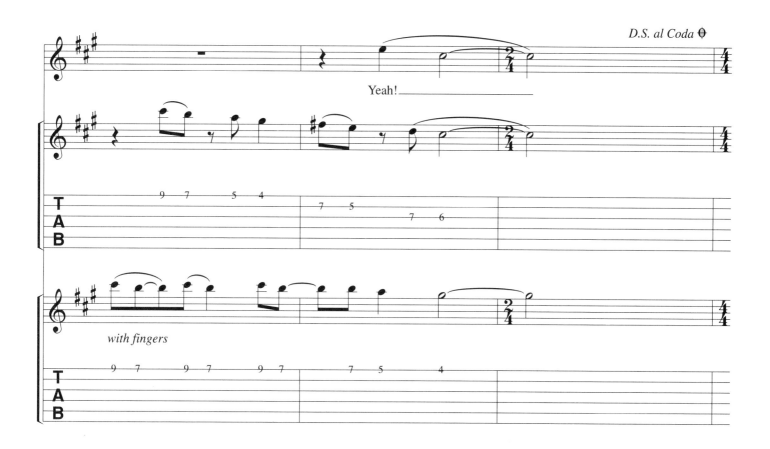

D.S. al Coda ✛

Yeah!_____

with fingers

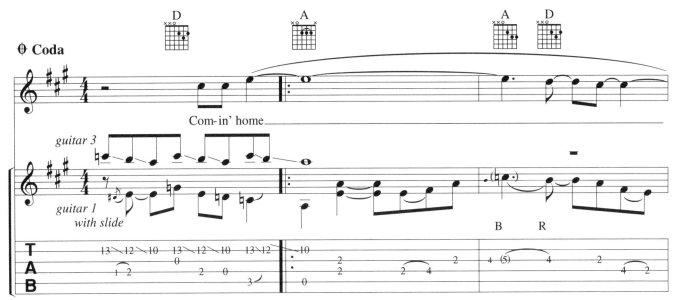

* guitar 2 resumes ad lib rhythm pattern

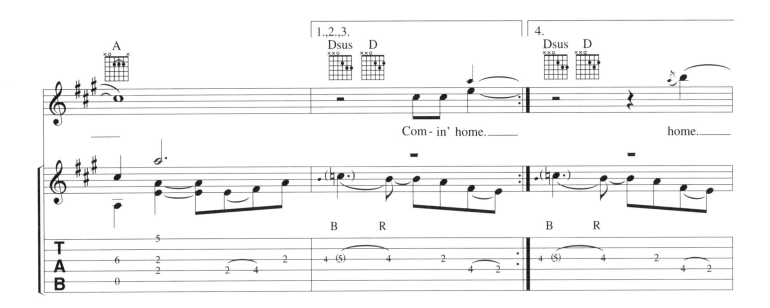

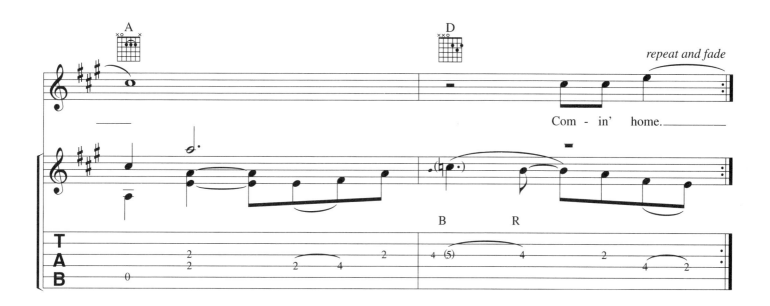

Keep On Growin'

Words and Music by Bobby Whitlock and Eric Clapton

*guitar 1 with fuzz

*Tune up ½ step:
①E♯ ②B♯ ③G♯
④D♯ ⑤A♯ ⑥E♯

guitar 1

* guitars 2&3 play ad lib fills

* guitars 2&3 continue simile

Chorus 1

grow - in',_____ a-keep on_____ grow - in',_____

a-keep on____ grow - in'._____

D.S. al Coda ⊕

2. I was

⊕ **Coda Pre-chorus 2**

guitar 1 Rhythm figure 3

She took my hand____ in hers____ and told my I____ was wrong.____

* guitars 2&3 continue simile

_____ She said,____ "You're gon - na be all____ right

boy____ Whoa,____ just as____ long"_____

Yes you did,

Aye,_____ hey,____ yeah,_____ yeah!"____

Oh, yes you did.

Got to keep on____

Chorus 2

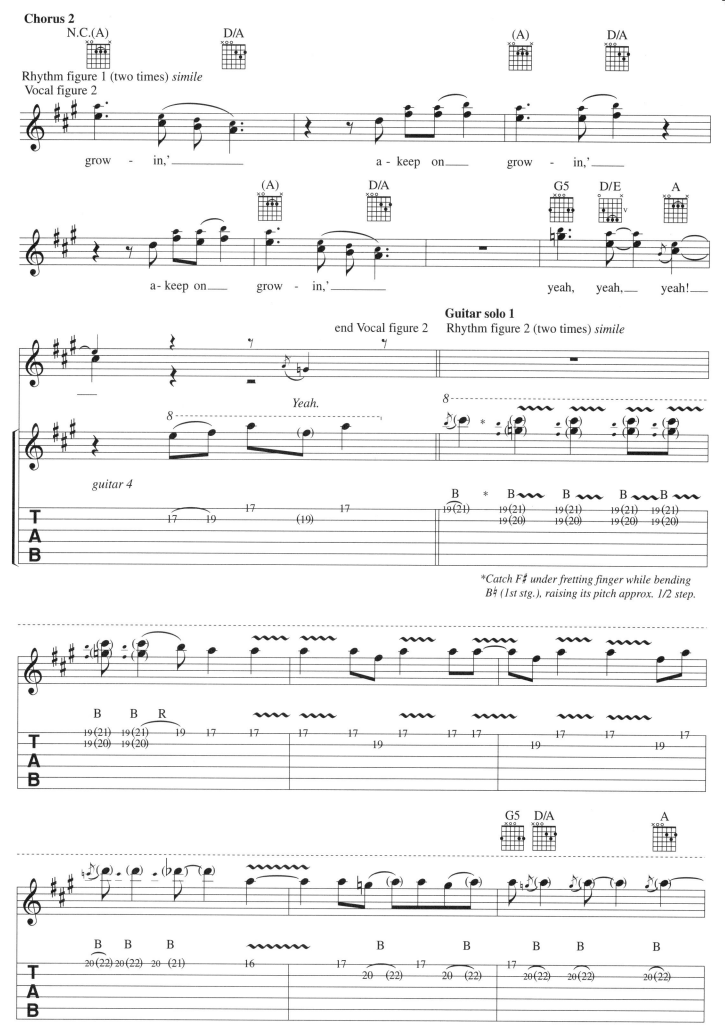

Catch F♯ under fretting finger while bending
B♮ (1st stg.), raising its pitch approx. 1/2 step.

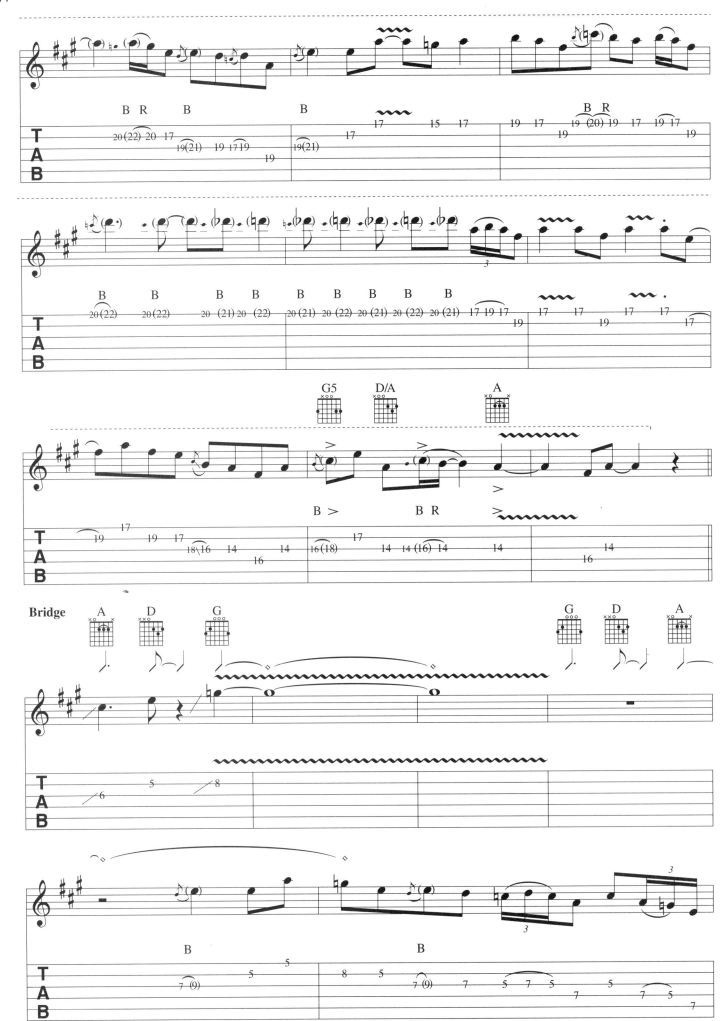

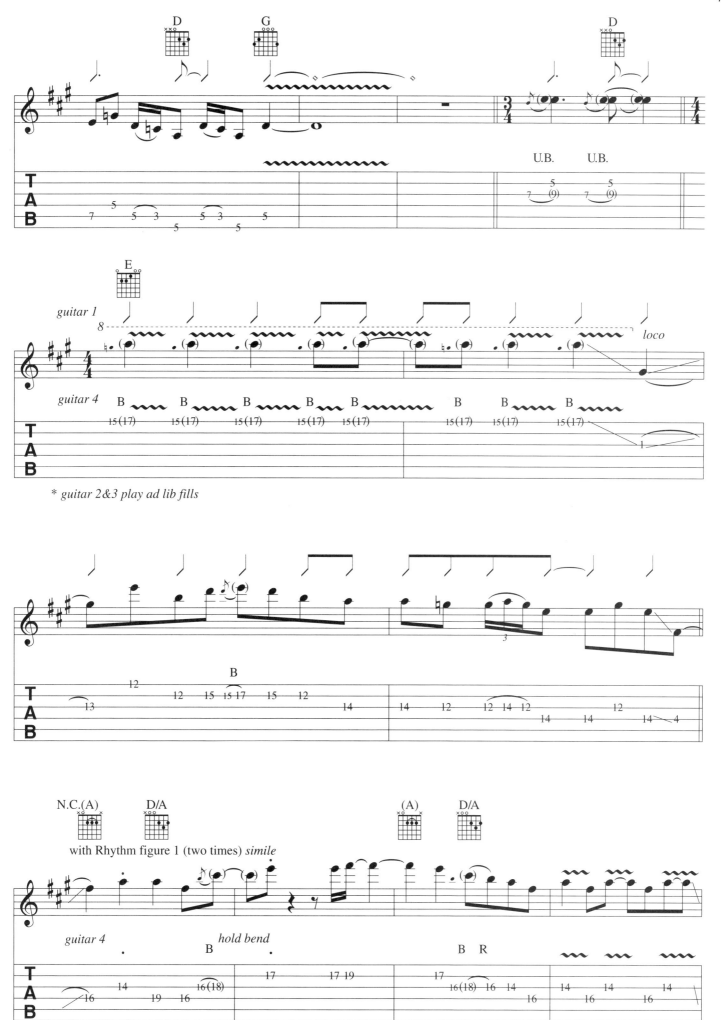

* guitar 2&3 play ad lib fills

guitars 2, 3, & 4 begin extended solo

Roll It Over

Words and Music by Eric Clapton and Bobby Whitlock

Bridge

You don't___ know how___ much it's means___ to be here in your arms.___ Roll it o-ver.

ver. Roll it o-ver.

Coda

Guitar solo

ver.

guitar 1 ** with Wah pedal

let ring

** Standard tuning
①E ②B ③G
④D ⑤A ⑥E

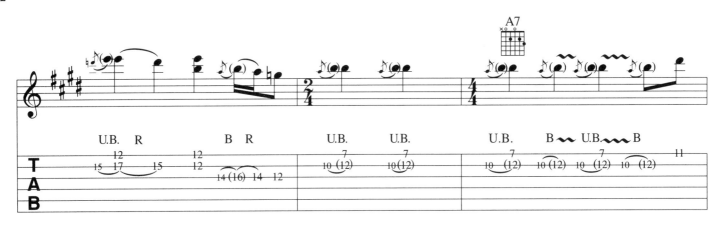

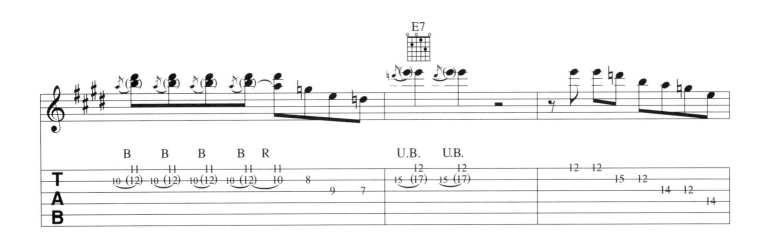

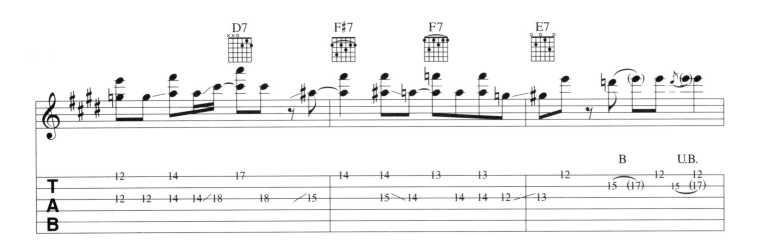

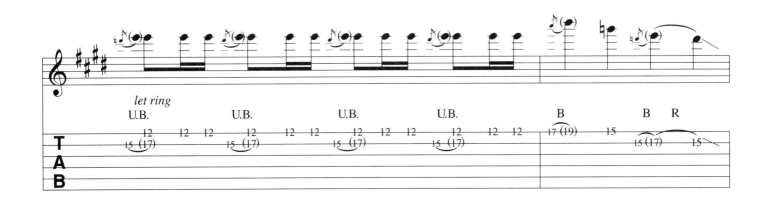

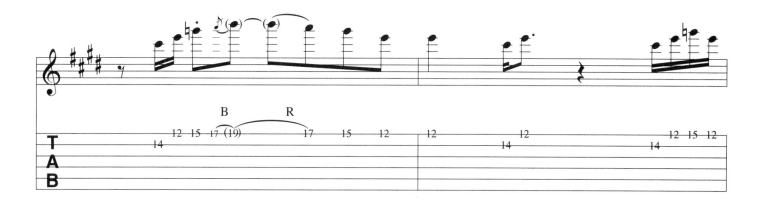

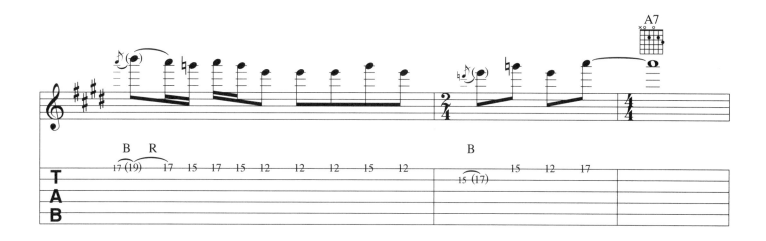

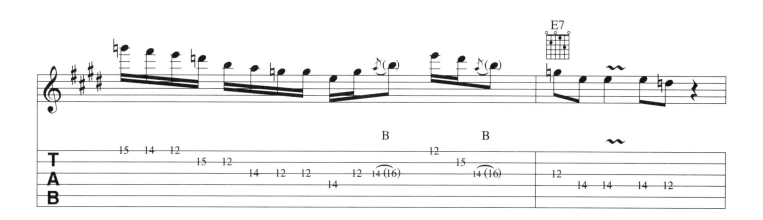

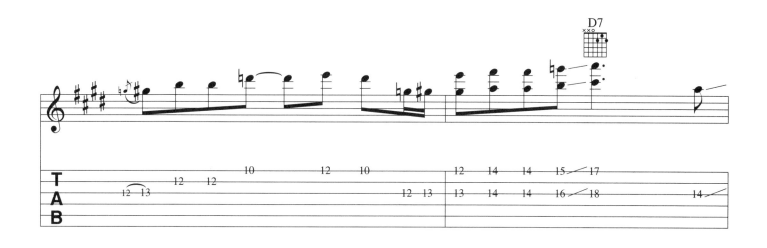

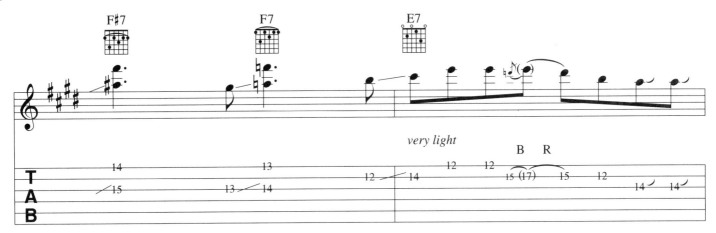

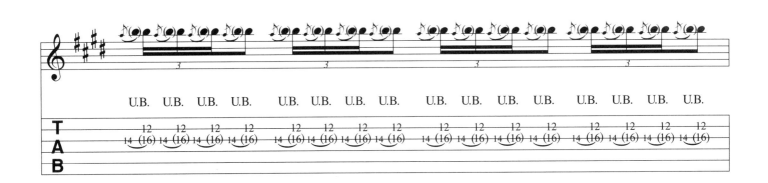

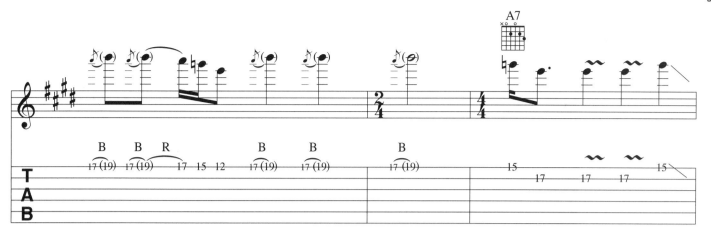

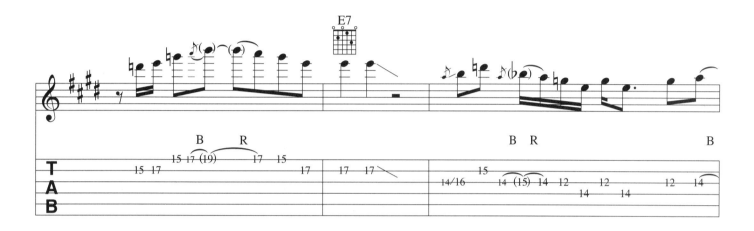

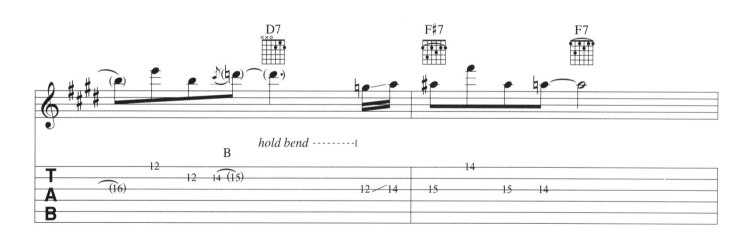

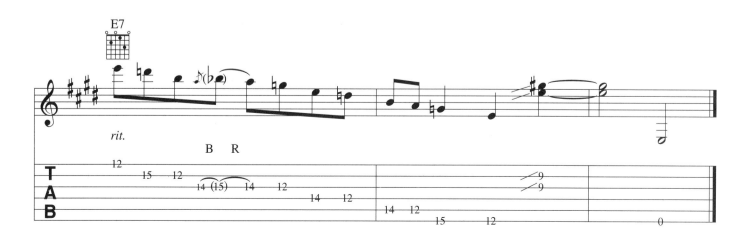

Let It Rain

Words and Music by Bonnie Sheridan and Eric Clapton

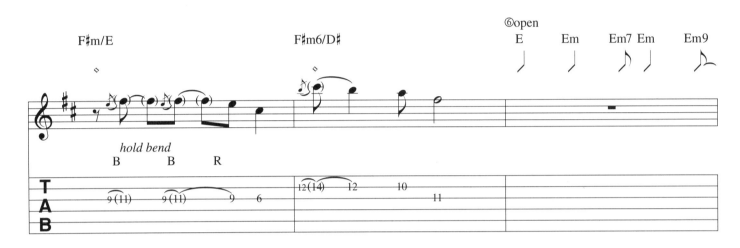

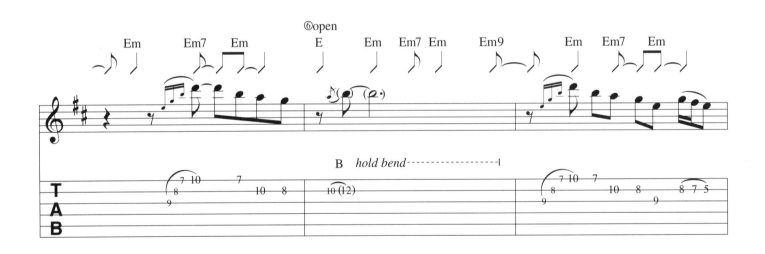

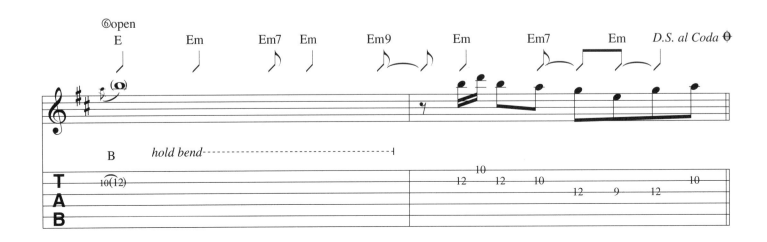

let it rain, rain, rain. Let it rain;

let it rain. Let your love rain down on me.

Let it rain; let it rain, Let it rain rain,

rain. (1st time only)

Rhythm figure 2

end Rhythm figure 2

Guitar solo 1
guitars 1 and 2 Rhythm figure 2 *simile*

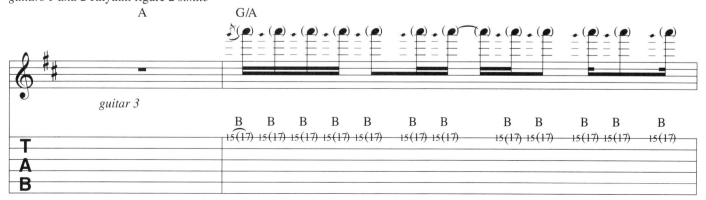

guitar 3

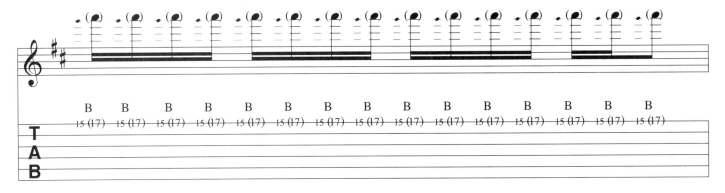

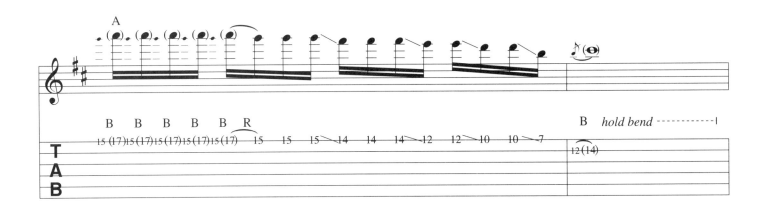

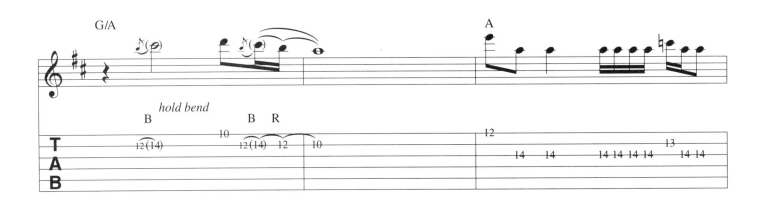

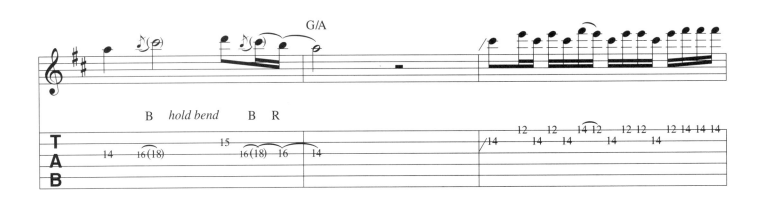

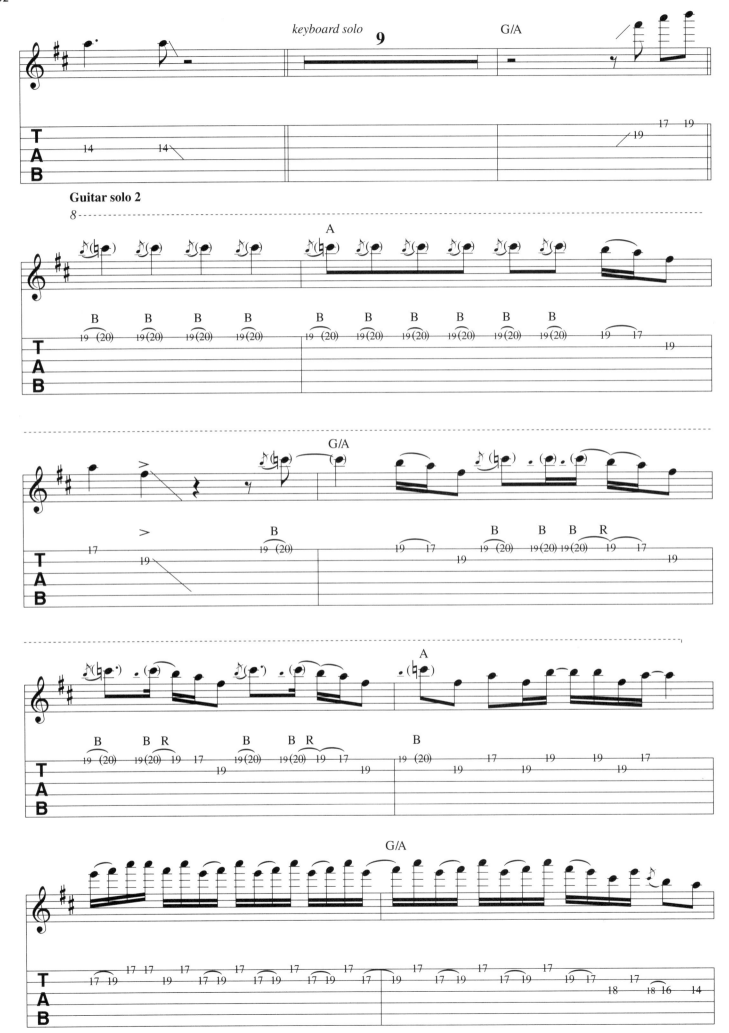

Guitar solo 2

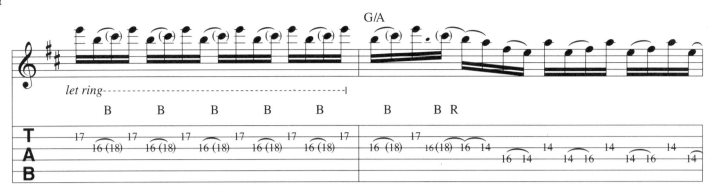

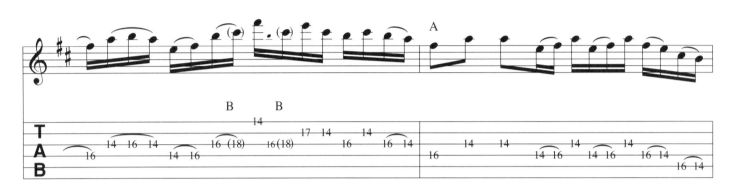